AF395675

Yoram Shalit ·
The European Powers' Plans regarding Jerusalem

ISLAMKUNDLICHE UNTERSUCHUNGEN · BAND 260

begründet
von
Klaus Schwarz

herausgegeben
von
Gerd Winkelhane

KLAUS SCHWARZ VERLAG · BERLIN 2004

ISLAMKUNDLICHE UNTERSUCHUNGEN · BAND 260

Yoram Shalit

The European Powers' Plans regarding Jerusalem towards the Middle of the 19th Century

KLAUS SCHWARZ VERLAG · BERLIN · 2004

Bibliografische Information Der Deutschen Bibliothek

Die Deutsche Bibliothek verzeichnet diese Publikation in der Deutschen Nationalbibliografie; detaillierte bibliografische Daten sind im Internet über http://dnb.ddb.de abrufbar.

© Gerd Winkelhane, Berlin 2004.
Klaus Schwarz Verlag GmbH, Postfach 41 02 40, D-12112 Berlin
ISBN 3-87997-316-4
Druck: Offsetdruckerei Gerhard Weinert GmbH, D-12099 Berlin

ISSN 0939-1940
ISBN 3-87997-316-4

To my wife Ofra

Contents

Abbreviations   4

1. The Place of Jerusalem and Palestine in European Politics   5

2. The Christian Churches in Jerusalem and Palestine and
   Their Place in International Politics   7

3. The Essence of European Plans   13

4. The Planners and their Plans   23

5. Rivalry Between France and the Holy See   43

6. Rumors about Occupation   53

Conclusion   59

Notes   61

Abbreviations

AE-	Archives des Affaires Etrangères, Paris
CC-	Correspondance Commercial, Ministère des Affaires Etrangères, Paris, Quai d'Orsay
CM-	Church Missionary Society, Birmingham University Library
EI-	*Encyclopaedia of Islam, 2nd Edition*
FO-	Foreign Office
MAE-	Archives de Ministère des Affaires Etrangères, Paris, Quai d'Orsay
n-	Note
PRO-	Public Record Office, Archives, London

Chapter 1

The Place of Jerusalem and Palestine in European Politics

Three spheres of relations and interests had a crucial influence on the policies of Russia, France, England, Prussia and Austria (the superpowers of that time). These spheres influenced their actual policies in the last quarter of the 18th and the first half of the 19th century, regarding the divisibility of the Ottoman Empire in general and the question of Jerusalem and the holy sites in particular. This influence was reflected in events like the Küçük Kaynārcı treaty, Napoleon's campaign in Egypt and Palestine, the Balkan uprisings, the rule of Mohammed Ali in Egypt, his son Ibrahim's Syrian campaign and the race for Jerusalem which is the focus of this essay.

The three spheres of influence can be loosely defined as:

1. The relations among the European powers themselves, based on their changing interests.

2. The relations between England and France, and the effects of these relations on the two countries' respective relations with Russia.

3. The "Eastern Question" and the European powers' interests in the Ottoman Empire.

Both Europe and the Ottoman Empire faced internal crisis during the 17th century, but in Europe the response to this crisis resulted in economic renaissance and technological progress which opened an era in which the European powers asserted their superiority over the Ottoman Empire at the turn of the 18th century.[1]

Chapter 2

The Christian Churches in Jerusalem and Palestine and Their Place in International Politics

1. The Greek Orthodox Patriarchate

The Greek Orthodox Church, and its patriarchate's unique rights in Jerusalem, was recognized by both the Muslim invaders and the Ottomans. The Ottomans corroborated ʿUmar ibn Al-Khattab's pledge in a special *ferman* issued by Sultan Selim I (1717), and in two additional *fermans* issued by Sultans Sulayman Kanun-i and Murad IV, on September 21, 1637.[2]

A Greek Orthodox patriarch representing the Church in Istanbul resided in Jerusalem throughout the Ottoman period. However, due to difficulties presented by the Wali, Kadi and Mufti, demands for bribery, and even threats to his life, he left for Istanbul leaving a deputy in his place, and returned only in 1844, as we shall see.[3]

2. The Latin (Catholic) Patriarchate

The Latin patriarchate was established in Jerusalem in 1099, immediately after the Crusaders' conquest of the city. When the Muslims retook Jerusalem in 1187, the Latin patriarch's residence was moved to Acre, and when the Muslims conquered Acre in 1291, the patriarch left the Holy Land. From that time until 1847, Jerusalem had no resident Latin patriarch, and the monks of the Franciscan order, who returned to Jerusalem in 1333, represented the pope in the city. In 1342 Pope Clement VI appointed them "Guardians of the Holy Places" (Custodia Terra Sancta), and they became the *de facto* legal authority over the remnants of Catholicism in Palestine. Even though they had not been charged with the task, they took it upon themselves to represent Catholic interests in the Holy Land.[4]

In the 19th century, especially following Ibrahim Pasha's campaign in Syria, the European powers began to take an interest in Palestine (European demands regarding the holy sites also intensified following the Treaty of Karlovitz of 1699, reflecting the weak position of the Ottoman Empire). We can say that at this point the issue of the holy sites began to be internationalized. This interest, born of strategic, political and religious considerations, resulted in the establishment of the Russian consulate in Jaffa in 1812, the appointment of British deputy-consuls in Haifa and Jaffa (under the General Consul in Alexandria), and the opening of

British and Prussian consulates in Jerusalem, in 1838 and 1842 respectively.[5]

In 1843, France reopened its consulate in Jerusalem, which had been closed at the beginning of the 18th century (1717). Sardinia also established a consulate in the city in the same year, and in 1847 Pope Pius IX sent a Latin patriarch to Jerusalem – the first such appointment for nearly 600 years. Some have suggested that this decision was made under French influence.[6]

At first glance, there seems to be nothing out of the ordinary in the appointments of the patriarch and French consul in Jerusalem. In 1830, the Sublime Porte issued a *ferman* recognizing freedom of faith for Catholics throughout the Ottoman Empire. This was an important turning point in the process by which the Catholic subjects of the Ottoman Empire withdrew from the patronage of the Greek Orthodox Church leaders.

Meanwhile, events in Syria during the years of Egyptian occupation hastened the official establishment of a Greek Catholic community. Thus, in 1838, Istanbul officially recognized both the freedom of the Catholic faith and its independence from Greek Orthodox authority. In other words, the Greek Catholic community, which had hitherto belonged to the Greek Orthodox *Millet*, was awarded the status of an independent *Millet*, with all pertaining rights including the appointment of patriarchs.[7]

The relationships among the various Christian communities in Jerusalem involved (both before and after this change) a unique element of controversy: the possession and use of Christianity's holy sites. Nor were European consuls an unusual phenomenon in the cities of the Levant, including Palestine. There had been a European presence there previously, and during the 18th century, including consuls and commercial representatives.[8]

However, we said "at first glance" because actually the appointments of the Latin patriarch and French consul definitely reflected new developments. In 1841, with Syria in crisis, Syrian Christians, probably inspired by missionaries, circulated a petition. It called *"for the object of requesting through their respective sovereigns or governments – that the Sublime Porte would grant the cession of Palestine, or that portion of Syria commonly denominated the Holy Land to all Christians, to be erected under the auspices of the Christian princes of Europe and Asia, into independent Christian territory, possessing self-government, and subjected to such a prince as the Christian nations may agree..."[9]*

This brings us to consider a link between the appointments and the petition.

In contrast to commercial interests, which had been the main cause for appointing consuls in the cities of Syria and the Levant in former centuries (apart from Jerusalem, where a French consul was already present from 1621 to 1717 charged by King Louis XIII with protecting the interests and safety of the Christian clergy),[10] the appointment of European consuls in Jerusalem from 1838 onwards was new in three respects. Firstly, the appointment was made after many years of absence; secondly, it was made for conceptual and ideological reasons incorporating the values of the French Revolution; thirdly, political intentions were concealed as religious motives. In the Jerusalem of this period there is no reason to look for economic motives.[11] The religious motive was part and parcel of the protectorate awarded to the Europeans over the various Christian communities, and associated with inter-Christian struggles over control of the Christian holy sites in Jerusalem.[12]

Chapter 3

The Essence of European Plans

The formal legal basis for the plans of the European powers was provided by the Capitulations. The Capitulations gave France political, commercial and religious influence, which France took full advantage of, using each kind of influence separately or all together.

A close examination of the French Capitulations of 1604, 1673 and 1740 suggests that this protection was personal rather than territorial, as reflected in the excerpt which describes the protectorate as the *"protection of Christian pilgrims to Jerusalem and the monks dwelling there."* In other words, it was protection for pilgrims to Jerusalem, Jesuits and Capucins.[13] French subjects dwelling in the Empire were also granted the right to custody of the holy sites.[14] Moreover, this right did not refer to the precise literal meaning of the word "protection", but to the protection of the special privileges granted by the sultans. In no case did the sultans relinquish their sovereignty or the obligations that ensued from this sovereignty – the duty to protect the privileges they had granted of their own free will, and the duty to protect the recipients of these privileges.

These privileges did not include the right to exercise direct, real, effective protection,[15] because to do this they would have had to permit a physical military presence, which would have been detrimental to the sultans' institutional sovereignty. A review of England's Capitulations of 1675, the 1699 Treaty of Karlowitz, and the 1774 Treaty of Küçük Kaynārcı, also shows quite clearly that, from both the phrasing and legal aspects, these documents speak of the same personal, intangible protection, rather than territorial protection. A religious French protectorate over the Catholic subjects of the Porte (just like a Russian protectorate over the Greek Orthodox subjects) had existed in the Ottoman Empire for hundreds of years before this period. It was both an official and unofficial protectorate.

The official protectorate pertained to the foreign clergy, and was meant to guard their interests, the religious practices of the Latin community, and the holy sites. The unofficial protectorate which applied to Christian subjects of the Porte was not grounded in any diplomatic agreement between the Porte and France, or for that matter between the Porte and Russia.

As Ottoman power declined, the Empire recognized the *de facto* French monopoly on the protectorate (in this sense, over the Catholic subjects), even though this was, in fact, no more than a moral theoretic protectorate. This state of affairs persisted until the end of the 18th century. In reality, France could not physically protect its consuls in Jerusalem from the Ottoman Walis who ruled there.

In fact, French consuls who resided or stayed in Jerusalem were sometimes jailed, deported or forced to flee from the city's governors,[16] which confirms the conclusion that the right granted to France was the right to "protect" its privileges morally but not physically or directly. This conclusion is corroborated by first-hand French sources: French Consul Jean de Blacas who held the office in Jerusalem in 1713, reported that the holy sites were *"sous puissante et royale protection de leur majesté, les Français."* French Consul Gavreil Marie Jean Benoit de Lantivy who arrived in Jerusalem in 1843 also reported that he had been sent to Palestine to protect *"les droits et les intérêts des Chrétiens."*[17]

The presence of a consul and consulate in Jerusalem was not essential for the protectorate to be in effect. Catholics – both foreign and subjects of the Porte – were protected by it in any case. Was it the right to moral protection that interested the initiators and designers of the various plans? Because if so, what was the urgency of sending a consul to Jerusalem, and what, if anything, was new about this step?

The European powers that were granted a protectorate, a theoretical and moral one, usually desired influence. In Jerusalem, during the period under discussion, these aspirations were manifested in increased activity, mostly on the part of Russia, for promoting Orthodox interests in the Porte's court, expanded Russian activities within the Greek Orthodox community, and a Russian missionary delegation. In addition, the various European powers supported their respective "protégé" communities in their quarrels with other communities over control and ownership of the Christian holy sites.

The powers' need to guard their interests at close hand, with the excuse of "protecting" their protégées and those protégés' rights, hastened the appointment of the consuls, and the planning of projects for the holy sites and Jerusalem. Plans were devised by Prussia, Russia, England, France and the Holy See.

When we examine the essence of the plans and the involvement of the powers in their preparation, we cannot escape the conclusion that there was a direct and close link between involvement in Jerusalem and involvement in the "Eastern Question" in general. While Oded Peri claims, in his book *Christianity under Islam in Jerusalem*, that since the 17th century, the sultan's policy towards the holy sites reflects the relations with the Europeans powers,[18] we think that the European policy reflects the inter-European relations and the treaties system.

Thus their policy in Jerusalem cannot be viewed as a separate policy, but rather as derived from their policy on the "Eastern Question".

We find this is true also regarding relations between consuls in Jerusalem. From 1845, relations between the French and British consuls were good, while relations were not good with the Russian and Austrian consuls because of Napoleon III's intervention in the process of Italian independence.[19] This conclusion is based on the following arguments:

1. Before Ibrahim Pasha's conquest of Syria, the powers showed no especial interest in Palestine and Jerusalem, and did not even have consuls in Jerusalem. Moreover, there had never been a French trading post (*echelle*) in Jerusalem. Between 1624-1717, French consuls resided in the city intermittently, all accountable to the consul in Sidon who bore the title of *"His Majesty's Consul in Palestine, the Galilee, Samaria, Jerusalem and Syria"*.

The post of the French consul in Jerusalem was abolished in the early 1800s because the sultans did not want a consulate in the city. They claimed Jerusalem was sacred to Islam, and the presence of a foreign Christian personage would eventually provide a basis for a Christian element in the city, which they did not want.

French economic (trading) interest in the Levant changed direction at this time, a change to which Dahir al-'Umar and Al-Jazzār also contributed by banishing the

French merchants from Acre. This was another reason – though not the main one – for the fact that no French consul was sent to Jerusalem until 1843. In 1839, Russian Consul Bazli also left Jaffa, after residing there for only one year, and moved to Beirut, though he visited Jerusalem from time to time.[20]

2. The quarrels and disputes among the Christian communities in Jerusalem began many years earlier. At the time, the European powers did not intervene directly. They only acted through diplomatic channels in the court of the Sublime Porte in Istanbul, using their political influence. This influence varied, and was based on the Capitulations, and on military and political assistance to the sultan, as he fought various wars, or combated threats to his rule.[21] In other words, the European powers engaged in diplomatic activity and lobbying on behalf of their protégées, but did not make any initiatives to alter their status in Jerusalem.

3. The number of Catholics in Jerusalem during the period under discussion varied from 200 to 850, while in all of Palestine, including Jerusalem, they numbered only 4,000. As this was clearly an absurdly small number to warrant the appointment of a resident patriarch, this could not have been

the reason for such a level of involvement, but rather an excuse and pretext for intervention desired for other reasons.

4. Ibrahim's reforms during his reign in Syria changed the legal status of non-Muslims. He made members of all faiths equal before the law, and included their representatives in the "advising councils" (Majlis ash-shura). These reforms aroused anger, hostility and disquiet, and reflected social and religious animosity.

Ibrahim managed to prevent angry mobs from harming non-Muslims. However, the renewed Ottoman regime was unable to do this, inciting further agitation with the *hatt-i şerif* of November 3, 1839, and the *hatt-i hümayun* of December 18, 1856.[22] These reactions compelled the European powers to exercise their protectorate over the non-Muslims, and intervene. Historians do not dispute the link between their intervention there and their position on the "Eastern Question".[23]

Thus we must examine in their entirety the European powers' policies toward the disintegrating Ottoman Empire, its preservation or alternatively its division, and the issue of Jerusalem in relation to this.

The policy of each of the powers stemmed from their own specific interests, and was aimed at neutralizing or balancing the policies of their allies and opponents. When Ibrahim conquered Syria and advanced toward Anatolia, France looked away or even showed sympathy, while

Russia came to the sultan's assistance and gained political benefits in the Unkiar Iskelesi Treaty (1833), which enabled the closing of the straits according to Russian demands. Then England, fearing Egyptian control of the land route to India, acted to neutralize Russia by joining it against Muhammad Ali, and in 1839, 1840 and 1841 they both neutralized France, who supported Muhammad Ali. They did this by including Prussia in the treaty for peace in the Levant, by the "Straits Covenant" for maintaining the Empire, and by the withdrawal of the Egyptian army from Syria and Palestine. France understood the threat to its interests, and joined the treaty in order to neutralize both Russia and England.[24] These European politics were manifested in the Crimean War (1854-1856), a war which clearly showed how the holy sites in Jerusalem were the catalysts for war, but not the motive, cause or reason for it.[25]

From this it may be concluded that the Empire's impending disintegration and the fear that one or another of the European powers would dominate, as well as the danger to the inter-community balance following Ibrahim's reforms and the antagonism they created toward the non-Muslims, were factors that aroused the European Powers' interest in Jerusalem. The quarrels among the various religious elements also contributed to this interest.

However, all of these merely served as a pretext for focusing the attention. The real motive was the apprehension that the entire region might fall under the influence of another power (European or Egyptian), and the desire to prevent this from happening. It may thus be concluded that the main concern for the powers was not the inhabitants, but rather the territory – quite the opposite of the original intent and spirit of the relevant sections of the Capitulations which they had requested and received.

Chapter 4

The Planners and Their Plans

Rome and France were not the first to devise plans regarding the holy sites. Prussia preceded them.

In February 1841, a petition from Christian inhabitants of Syria was sent to the representatives of the five powers in Istanbul, calling on the large Christian states to intervene in the affairs of Syria and save Holy Palestine from the Turks.[26] Another local petition was addressed to a religious personage – the pope – asking him to appoint a Latin patriarch who would reside in Jerusalem. The petition stated that this was also the desire of the inhabitants of Syria.[27]

In other words, not only did the actions of the European powers precede those of the Church, but the local population also approached the powers before approaching the pope. The European initiatives did indeed precede the petitions, but the local conditions were undoubtedly ripe to receive them. These conditions helped to ensure local cooperation, and highlighted the distress of the Christian communities. The fact that no direct petition was presented to France may be explained by the probability that the local Christian population was not unaware of current events in European politics, and understood France's paradoxical situation with the Porte, in the light of French support for Muhammad Ali.

As Muhammad Ali's ally, France was neutralized and left out of the initiative discussed below. On February 24, 1841, Prussia presented a proposal to the four powers of the "Holy Alliance" (Austria, Great Britain, Russia and Prussia). It suggested that they should come to an agreement amongst themselves, and with France as well, to henceforth protect the cities of Jerusalem, Bethlehem and Nazareth from the indignity and disgrace brought upon them by Turkish rule, and defend the Christian dwellers of these cities against Muslim fanaticism.

According to their proposal,

1. The Christian population of these cities, the churches and monasteries, the hospitals and their dependants, the pilgrims, scholars, craftsmen and temporary Christian residents who suffered from the intervention of the Turkish authorities in their internal affairs would all be excluded from Turkish jurisdiction.

2. The Christian residents of these cities would no longer be included in the *"ra'aya"* (protégé) category. From now on

they would be considered, in the narrow legal view of their person and property, as subjects of the five European powers. Commitment to the Porte would be communal rather than personal.

3. The title to the holy sites in Jerusalem, Bethlehem and Nazareth would be transferred to the five Christian powers, according to a special agreement with them.

4. Christians residing in these cities, either permanently or temporarily, would be considered separate entities according to their various sects and customs of worship. Each entity would be considered a separate, officially recognized community. The right to use the holy sites would be determined. The English community would be allowed to worship in its own manner and establish a hospital. Its members would be permitted to hold their ceremonies in the Church of the Holy Sepulchre and the Basilica of Bethlehem, in special places allotted to them.

5. The site of the old Temple Mount and the Mosque of ʿUmar would in any event remain in the hands of the Turks.

6. Three Christian communities, the Greek Orthodox, the Catholics and the Protestants, would be ruled by three European commissioners, each commanding a military force

of 60 soldiers. France and Austria would appoint a commissioner for ruling over the Catholics, Russia would appoint a commissioner for conducting the affairs of the Greek Orthodox, and Prussia and England would appoint a commissioner for the Protestant community.[28]

A close analysis of the proposal's contents reveals that the Prussians proposed a guardianship of both the Christians and the holy sites. Thus they expand the Capitulations, by proposing territorial custody in addition to personal guardianship.

Moreover, we have here a proposal for changing the status of the sultan's Christian subjects from *"ra'aya"* to subjects of the five powers, transference of titles to the holy sites in Jerusalem, Bethlehem and Nazareth to the five powers, and the appointment of European commissioners for the three Christian communities.

The content of this proposal has very profound significance. Not only do the powers actually expropriate these cities and their Christian inhabitants from the Ottomans and turn them into extra-territorial subjects – the proposal has another feature which is more important for our discussion. Joint management means mutual neutralization of the powers, as well as mutual recognition of each power's right to maintain a presence in the holy sites. This right was more important to the powers than guardianship of these cities' residents.

Prussia did not only act with regard to the political aspects of Palestine and the holy sites as part of a political plan. It also acted out of religious motives intertwined with the other motives of the February 1841 proposal mentioned above. The Prussian king, Frederick William IV, proposed that the Anglican Church should establish an English diocese in Jerusalem. This proposal may have arisen from the impossibility of implementing the political proposal, as we shall see later on, first and foremost because of Russia's objections. In effect, this meant joining the establishment of the Anglican Church on Mount Zion, associated with the London Society for Promoting Christianity among the Jews, which Frederick William IV viewed as the beginning of a new era for the Protestant Church.

Indeed, he did not express his enthusiasm for sending a Bishop to Jerusalem in words only, but in a generous financial contribution as well. The Prussian king considered the increased Protestant activity in Jerusalem to be a tool for reinforcing the Protestant Church and spreading it among the primitive Christian believers. It would justify the Protestant Church in the eyes of the Eastern churches, converting them by the sheer force of pure faith and example, and present a Church united in the eyes of its leaders.[29]

Russia refused the Prussian proposal and introduced one of its own on March 11, 1841. The ten-item proposal was presented to the four other powers. Its main points were:

1. The existing situation in Palestine would be preserved; namely, Palestine would remain under Ottoman sovereignty, as a separate governing unit, answerable directly to the "Porte", and not to the Wali of Damascus or any other authority.

2. A new *Hatt-i şerif* would be published, corroborating those published in the past in favor of Jerusalem's Church and clergy.

3. An Ottoman governor would be appointed for Palestine, a man of conscience and justice who would reside in Jerusalem or Jaffa and preside over a civil system and military power sufficient for keeping order and guarding the holy sites from desecration by the Bedouins of the desert.

4. Quarrels among the local clergy of the various Christian communities would be forbidden. They would not be allowed to engage in "childish disputes" or to level "false accusations" against each other. The status quo among the communities and titles to the holy sites, as determined in the royal decrees, would be preserved.

5. The Mufti and Kadi of Jerusalem would not be permitted to cheat and demand gifts (bribes) from the Christian clergy and heads of the monasteries whenever they approached a local judicial authority or sought to free themselves from certain taxes.

6. Fear of taxes, cheating and bribery demands had caused the patriarchs of Jerusalem to depart for Istanbul some time ago, and leave the management in the hands of deputies. This decree would be a wise act, enabling the present patriarch to return.

7. All amendments regarding the ancient hierarchy of the Eastern Church would be rejected as dangerous and inapplicable, and all demands for priority or privileges on the part of the other religious communities would only be accepted after a just, honest, in-depth examination. A special tribunal acting as an advisory committee would examine such cases. The tribunal would consist of the district's Wali, the patriarch of Jerusalem (or his deputy in his absence), the head of the Latin faiths, the head of the Armenian Church, and a special *ad hoc* supervisor, chosen and appointed by the Supreme Porte from among the reputable bishops of the Greek community in Istanbul.

8. Repairs of churches and monasteries damaged by time and events would be permitted and approved by the local authorities each time the leaders of these communities request permission, and the governor would not require gifts or permit fees on these occasions.

9. The Turkish soldiers guarding the gates of the church enclosing the Church of the Holy Sepulchre would not be allowed to enter the church on the pretense of maintaining order. The soldiers would also respect the instructions of the patriarch and his messengers.

10. As for the Russian pilgrims who came to the holy sites every year, the Supreme Porte would order its civilian clerks and military officers to give them all possible protection and assistance. In order to ensure that these foreign visitors and travelers, who generally did not speak the local language, would not be exposed to taxes and other obstacles, his Honor the Consul residing in Jaffa would have the authority, whenever he saw fit, to accompany the convoy of his nation's pilgrims during their stay in Jerusalem.[30]

Clauses 5-6 help us understand what really stood behind Russia's rejection and its revised proposal. The Greek Orthodox patriarch had previously left Jerusalem and moved to Istanbul precisely because of these taxes and expenses, as well as the threat to his personal safety. This clause would enable him to return to Jerusalem.[31] The cover story for his return was the need for preserving law and order. The true intention, however, was reinstating the title rights and supremacy of the Greek Orthodox Church; title rights that they claimed had been grounded in the sultans' *fermans* since 1517 – when the first sultan had declared his commitment to the edict issued by the Khalif ʿUmar Ibn Al-Khattab.[32] In other words, the Russians preferred to preserve the status quo alone, without joint administration, because this would enable them to act freely in Jerusalem, without the watchful supervision of their partners in the administration.

As for England, it began to develop a relationship with Jewish residents in Jerusalem about a hundred years before the Balfour Declaration. Here also we find the link between political interests and cultural-ideological values, but for the British, unlike the French, these were very powerful religious values. As with the French, though somewhat later, this issue takes us back to the beginning of the 18th century.[33] There were four different aspects to the English plan:

1. A Jewish entity under Ottoman sovereignty would strengthen the sultan and the Empire economically, while neutralizing French aspirations regarding their support of Muhammad Ali.

2. Love of the Bible prevailed in England, and the British plan, unlike the French, had definite religious facets. The dream was to establish sovereignty over a Christian-Jewish entity, with a British protectorate under Ottoman sovereignty.

3. Economic interests in preserving the land passage to India where the French were challenging British domination.

4. The idea of converting the Jews to Protestant Christianity under the British protectorate.

This spurred the French to appoint a French consul in Jerusalem. France could not remain indifferent and leave Jerusalem open to increased Russian or British activity. Among those superpowers, France was the only one who had supported, taken steps and acted towards a separate and independent entity in Palestine during the previous 100 years, as can be seen in the following events:

1. ʿAli Bey al-Kabir's campaign in Palestine and Syria in 1771.

2. Napoleon's campaign in Palestine.

3. Ibrahim Pasha's campaign in Palestine and Syria.

4. The appointment of a French consul to Jerusalem in 1843 and the protectorate plan.

Throughout the 19th century, the basic French policy regarding the "Eastern Question" was guarding the Ottoman Empire against encroachment by the powers of the Holy Alliance. Its policy in Jerusalem was motivated by the opposite interest – to establish French domination in the Mediterranean. The contradiction of fortifying the Empire's position on the one hand, and establishing French domination on the other, was settled through opposition to the actual elimination of the Empire, and support for the policy of Muhammad Ali in Syria and Egypt. The Latins, protected by France in Jerusalem, derived immediate benefits from this support, obtaining several privileges in the holy sites in Jerusalem at the expense of the Greek Orthodox.[34]

At the same time, and for the same reason, France invaded Ottoman Algiers in 1830, thereby opening a period of colonialization in North Africa, which reinforces the assumptions made regarding its real intentions in Jerusalem.[35] Despite the fact that France, unlike the other European states, supported Muhammad Ali, paradoxically these countries had consular representation in Palestine and Jerusalem while France did not.

This may be explained by changes in French economic interests in the Levant, or by the separation between state and religion and the long internal struggle during the first half of the 19th century between the Republicans and supporters of the Church. This was a struggle over internal French issues and relationships with the pope and the resulting depreciation in the amount of attention paid to the holy sites.[36]

France's protégées paid the price for this double-edged policy. When Muhammad Ali retreated, they were forced to immigrate from Asian *Wilayets* (provinces), including Palestine, fearing the retaliation of the renewed Ottoman regime. As a result, France had to consolidate and reshape its position in the East, especially in the holy sites.

Therefore France sought to appoint a consul with suitable capabilities, who was well acquainted with the East. The man chosen for the job was Gavriel Marie Jean de Lantivy – by no means an innocent appointment. According to his own report, he was sent to Palestine to protect the rights and interests of the Christians – *"pour y défendre les droits et les intérêts des Chrétiens"*.[37]

Whose rights exactly? The interests of which Christians? Those residing in Jerusalem, subjects of the sultan, or European Christians? Or perhaps French Christians, in the sense that guarding the right to protection is interpreted as a means for influencing and acting within the Catholic population? As the original source states: *"de conserver un droit de protection, c'est à dire un moyen d'influence et d'action sur les nombreuses populations catholiques"*.[38]

When the new consul spoke in 1843 of "protecting the rights" he probably meant protecting the rights of the French to protect the right of the Latins to protect the holy sites.[39] Once again we see that the issue is not possession of territory, but rather the status of those protecting the rights of the Latins in the holy sites.

During this time, France's intention to establish a "religious" -secular protectorate in Jerusalem coincided with the pope's intention to appoint a patriarch for that city. However, the intentions of the two were again in conflict over the question of who would be appointed to the respective positions. In this, France revealed motives that shed new light on the pope's position on this issue.

The appointment of a Latin patriarch was not a French initiative. The idea of appointing a Catholic bishop in Jerusalem circulated around the court of the Holy See as early as January 1842, in reaction to the appointment of an Anglican bishop in the city. The French knew nothing of these ideas. Rome did not coordinate its positions with Paris, and the French learned about the papal intent only through a report from the French ambassador in Rome to his superior in Paris, Foreign Minister Guizot.[40]

In other words, the idea arose in Rome quite independently of any French involvement, and no Church official informed the French of it. Moreover, an examination of the chronology reveals that such ideas had already appeared in Rome a year before the reopening of the French consulate and the appointment of the French consul in Jerusalem in 1843.

This does not mean that notions about opening a consulate in Jerusalem were not heard in Paris at the time. Quite the contrary. The idea of appointing a consul in Jerusalem came up in Paris and Rome simultaneously. Paris also did not inform Rome of its plans and intentions.[41] However, Paris was more practical and more decisive than Rome in carrying out its plans, partly because it experienced no internal power struggles or conflicting interests on this issue.

Anglican activity was not the only thing that worried the Holy See. The pope was even more troubled by increased Russian diplomatic activity in the court of the Porte, in favor of the Greek Orthodox Church, and in Jerusalem through the Russian Mission, combined with the return of a local origin (Lydia) Greek patriarch to Jerusalem in 1844.[42]

Rome's guiding principle was the desire to prevent the accelerated growth of heresy and factionalism that threatened Catholicism in Jerusalem, which was partly the result of this active competition. The appointment of a Latin patriarch in Jerusalem seemed like an appropriate solution.[43]

This is when the Holy See began to devise plans for Jerusalem, and where its interests intersected with French policy.

Various ideas circulated in the papal court, some of which may be understood to express political and religious designs on Palestine. Most of these were never implemented, but the French consul in Rome called them "dreams" and "crazy plans." In his report he mentioned two of them:

1. Establishing an independent state in Palestine based on the aristocracy of both a military and a religious order.

2. Founding a hereditary or elected monarchy in Jerusalem.[44]

These plans are reminiscent of the Crusader Kingdom of Jerusalem.[45] At first glance it may seem strange that the French government was not involved in the plans, but only informed of them. In 1843 the more practical plans and interests of the Holy See coincided with those of France. These were intended to counterbalance and deter the efforts of the competitors, Russia and Great Britain, in Jerusalem. Rome saw two possible courses of action:

1. To establish a patriarchy, or at least appoint a Latin patriarch in the Holy Land, to guard the unity of the various Catholic factions, and guide them in a common direction.

2. To send well-known clergymen with elevated religious standing to Palestine, who would outclass the Franciscan elite, or at least initiate reform among the Franciscans, who were the *de facto* representatives of the Catholic position and interests in the Holy Land.[46]

These plans were clearly disproportionate to the number of Catholics in Jerusalem, and did not specify a role for the French consul.

The French plan was similar, only more ambitious, with an emphasis on French dominance and political goals in Palestine. As we shall see, France was not content with a moral theoretical protectorate. It sought a practical, active and political protectorate. France set goals that were not shaped during the period under discussion, but quite a few years earlier. Documents from 1790, found in the Marseilles archives, contain a large dose of the term *"Colonie Française"*, pertaining to Egypt and Syria. It appears that Napoleon's Syrian campaign was launched when he interpreted Syrian-Palestinian politics and the local revolts as the rebellions of nations oppressed by the Ottomans. He regarded this as an opportunity for permanent French settlement in Egypt and for uniting with the Eastern population.[47]

Henry Laurens defined Napoleon's aim as the desire to establish *"une colonie franco-arabe"*. Hence the question arises, did Napoleon's dreams sow the seeds for the French plans under discussion?

Another possibility is the connection between political interests and plans and a value-oriented, ideological aspect – namely, that political acts are usually accompanied by supporting values. This possibility may be discerned in Napoleon's proclamation to the People of Egypt, and – more relevant to this discussion – in his proclamation to the People of Israel.[48] When Napoleon invaded Palestine and reached Acre, he did not do so for religious reasons. It was an "offensive act of defense", since this was a vital position for French domination of Egypt.[49]

It may also be assumed, though without sufficient proof, that his plans were inspired by former rulers of Egypt ᶜAli Bey and Abu 'dh-Dhahab, the Egyptian Mamluks who conquered Palestine in order to link Egypt with Syria, taking advantage of the central government's weakness.

Napoleon may also have derived the inspiration for approaching the inhabitants of Jerusalem from ᶜAli Bey. ᶜAli Bey needed a great deal of money plus Russian support for his Syrian campaign. German officers who served in the Russian fleet that docked at the harbor of Livorno in 1781, and who knew ᶜAli Bey personally, mediated between him and the wealthy members of the Jewish community there. ᶜAli Bey agreed, for a sum of money, to take Jerusalem and give it to the Jewish people (*"für einen gewissen Preis Jerusalem der Jüdischen Nation zu überlassen"*).[50]

Moreover, the Coptic *dragoman* who assisted Napoleon was well acquainted with the declarations of ᶜAli Bey and Hasan Pasha. Napoleon himself did not even bother to visit Jerusalem. The proclamation he issued on April 20, 1799, did not address the Jews of Palestine or Jerusalem, but rather "All the Jews of the East ... not to conquer the land of your forefathers but for you to receive with the support of this [the French] nation and under its assurance, that which has already been conquered to demand and assert your political existence as a nation among nations, and the natural unrestricted right to worship the Lord in accordance with your faith." Unlike the proclamation in Egypt, this proclamation was not intended for the local population, but for all the People of Israel. The proclamation offered the Jews the territory already occupied, with the support and assurance of the French nation.

Thus, the proclamation did not speak of permanent French settlement in Palestine, but neither did it explicitly mention a state or an entity, an autonomy or a national home, concepts which at the time were anyway rather obscure. The entire subject was vague, and perhaps the words *"support and assurance"* meant in fact a French protectorate.[51] It is worth adding that Napoleon spread the values of the French Revolution, and called on the People of Israel, not the Jews residing in Palestine, to rally round his flag.

In fact, he intended to establish an Arab entity under his protectorate, through which he could reach India. As mentioned above, Napoleon's actions had no religious motives, as he was not a religious man. Even in his proclamation to the People of Egypt he appeared more Muslim than the Mamluks. His faith had no significance, and this is how his approach to the People of Israel should also be viewed.

If we accept the hypothesis that "Muhammad Ali was for the French a kind of Eastern Napoleon over whom France desired a protectorate, and therefore supported",[52] we may conclude that when France proposed the establishment of a "religious" (meaning secular and political) French protectorate in the Levant, it was continuing a traditional French policy.

In the period under discussion, this policy takes on the unusual characteristic of vigorous action towards expanding French cultural influence by increasing cultural activity within the non-Muslim population. The French consul in Jerusalem, Gavriel Marie Jean de Lantivy, in his letter to the French foreign minister, revealed the immediate goals of the general French policy: "...*La politique généreuse de la France tend à amener dans ces contrées, l'ordre, la paix, la lumière tous les bienfaits de la civilisation.*" Or, in free translation, "generous French policy desires to bring to these regions arrangements of peace, enlightenment/culture, and all the benefits of civilization".[53] It was Foreign Minister Guizot who introduced the new policy and defined it as a "French offensive in the name of Christian Civilization interests" which means that the idea of Christian civilization now precedes the idea of the French Revolution.[54]

Moreover, from now on there is a significant change in French perception, as in the perception of other powers, regarding the protectorates issue. They are seen no longer as theoretical-moral protectorates, but active political protectorates. This change was partly the result of the sultan's inability to do his duty as a sovereign and protect his non-Muslim subjects effectively. *"Si le but de ces nobles efforts est d'assurer, aux Chrétiens une protection efficace, et à la Turquie une bonne administration"*. And if the purpose of these "noble efforts" was to ensure an effective protectorate for the Christians and a competent administration for the Turks, there was need for peace and harmony among the local communities.[55] Use of force to implement the protectorate was an option, either as a threat or in practice, although only as a last resort.[56]

Chapter 5

Rivalry Between the French and the Holy See

By giving a religious pretext, France could expect the support of the Holy See for the French protectorate in the Levant. Rome could not ignore the fact that the lives of Catholics there were threatened due to the disruption of the inter-community balance following Muhammad Ali's reforms and the renewed Ottoman regime. In other words, at this stage, the French plan coincided with the immediate papal interest of protecting the lives of Catholics. The Church had no operative power, and was totally dependent on France in this matter. When France established a consulate in Jerusalem and sent a consul there, the pope would recognize France's determination, as well as the potential of these acts to further Catholic interests.[57]

France, then, could expect to gain papal recognition for the entity that it wished to establish. And indeed, in Rome, where the idea of appointing a bishop in Jerusalem met with opposition, the French ambassador was told that the idea of appointing a French consul in

Jerusalem would be viewed favorably. Moreover, the pope even proposed candidates, and expressed his opinions on the future consul's desirable qualifications.

On February 25, 1842, the French ambassador in Rome reported this to Foreign Minister Guizot, adding a description of the appropriate qualities of the appointed consul as desired by the Court of the Holy See: "It is very important that Jerusalem should be given to a person who is well acquainted with the East, and convinced of the importance and love of the need to protect the interests of the clergy and the Catholic population against the threatening enemies."[58]

This means that the ideas and thoughts arose simultaneously in Rome and in Paris, without prior consultation. It was not a joint, coordinated plan, but an attempt to influence the French may be discerned, and also vice versa, as we shall see.

At this stage, both the French and papal plans were merely theoretical. Then the French began to take steps to appoint a consul in Jerusalem. Usually, French consuls were authorized to act in the cities in which they officiated. The French consul appointed in Jerusalem in 1843 was aware of his government's protectorate plan, and in a letter to his foreign minister from July 12, 1843, he suggested that the authority of the consul and consulate in Jerusalem should apply not only to the city of Jerusalem, but also "to a territory that corresponds with the territory of the Jerusalem Pashalık as it appears in the German map of Syria printed in Gotha in 1835." He pointed out that the motive and reason for his suggestion was that the consulate's protectorate would correspond with the territory of the Damascus Pasha, under whose authority it was located, and would thus be recognized by the Pasha.[59]

His argument may be viewed as simply pragmatic, but it may also have been influenced by awareness of his government's policies, both declared and undeclared. We can conclude that his proposal reflected the idea of a wider and political protectorate, not only the original personal one. Unlike France, the Holy See continued to deliberate about the appointment of a patriarch in Jerusalem. Not only did Rome and France act independently of one another, France also considered the appointment of a patriarch to be detrimental to its own plans, and instructed its ambassador in Rome to express its opposition to this idea to the Holy See.[60] There were several reasons for French opposition:

1. The appointment would not contribute to peace among the Catholics in Jerusalem, and would embarrass the consul.

2. The bishop might support the activities of the Austrians and Sardinians (who also had recently sent representatives to Jerusalem).

3. The consul would find it difficult to consolidate his own position, and worst of all, the appointment would obstruct the protectorate plan.[61]

The consul in Jerusalem supported this standpoint, which originated in Paris.[62]

The issue of appointing a patriarch in Jerusalem, and the question of who should be appointed to the position, had no simple solutions, due also to divisions within the Church. The Franciscans in Jerusalem, as a monastic order, opposed the moves of the Church and France; moves which, though uncoordinated, were liable to undermine their exclusive status in the holy sites, obstruct their "cultural" activities in the Holy Land, and make the Catholic population less dependent on them. As they acted to thwart the plans in the court of the Holy See, they also initiated confrontations with the French consul in Jerusalem, whom they viewed as a competitor. These activities proved harmful to the local Catholic population.[63]

Pope Pius IX ignored all opposition to the appointment of a patriarch, and in May 1847 he decided to reestablish the Latin patriarchate in Jerusalem. The decision was formally ratified on May 23, 1847.[64] Two months later France became aware of this. The decision caused concern in the French Foreign Ministry, and the ambassador in

Rome was told to be on guard, as it was perceived as an obstruction and danger to the French protectorate plan.[65]

It is not unlikely that the return of the Greek Orthodox patriarch from Istanbul to Jerusalem in 1844, after an absence of many years, was behind the pope's decision.[66] Now that the decision had been made, the question of who would be appointed to this important post arose once again.

There is no doubt that the French made considerable efforts to influence the choice of the man who would become the patriarch of Jerusalem. The ambassador in Rome received specific instructions to prevent the appointment of a Sardinian. *"Il est à désirer d'abord que ce ne soit pas un Sarde."*[67] France was very much in favor of the appointment of a French patriarch, or at least one approved by the French government.[68]

It was opposed to the appointment of a Sardinian for several reasons. While the French government strove to guard its secular interests in the East, it also struggled against the "Italian Revolution." The alliance between the pope and the king of Sardinia, arising from internal Italian considerations, was perceived as a withdrawal of papal support from the French protectorate.[69] This raises the question of why France cared so much about the identity of the appointed patriarch. Was it because French plans in Jerusalem differed from those of the pope, and France wanted an elected patriarch who would agree to the French plan?

Suspicions grow when we read the briefing given by the French foreign minister to his ambassador in Rome: "*Il est à désirer d'abord que ce ne soit pas un Sarde: et vous devriez agir, confidentiellement au besoin pour que cela ne le fût pas. Il serait superflu de vous dire les raisons. Vous les connaissez parfaitement: il ne me reste qu'à recommander cette affaire à toute votre vigilance.*"[70] During the period under discussion, France shifted the emphasis of its activities to the Sultan's non-Muslim subjects, at the expense of the foreigners, the missionaries. France realized that by strengthening its position with the local population, it would gain politically.[71]

In this context the request presented by the Christians of the Levant to the European powers in 1841 should be mentioned, which coincided with the change in the French view of the protectorate.[72] There may also have been a link with the actual appointment of the French consul in Jerusalem. The pope did not give in to French demands. He proposed a "compromise candidate", and appointed Mgr. Joseph Valerga as patriarch, a Sardinian by birth, but residing in Rome and with Roman education and customs. France was informed that he had been given instructions to appease the interests of the French government.[73]

Before the days of Pope Pius IX, the Church's dealings with the Porte were conducted through the consuls of the Catholic countries. Pius IX changed the Holy See's approach to a "religious" French protectorate. This was a result of the independent policy and diplomacy he began to conduct with the Porte, whose purpose was to obtain a trade contract and normal relations. Possibly, the trade contract served as a facade for the intention to receive Capitulations that would grant the Holy See a protectorate over the Catholic Christians, similar to that given to the secular Christian states.[74]

This may be the answer to the question of the disproportion between the plan and the number of Catholics in Jerusalem and the reason why the pope did not give in to French pressure. The French, of course, were displeased. They understood that the pope's activities challenged their exclusive protectorate over the Catholic Christians, and even threatened the policy and plans of the French protectorate. But the French were not insistent. They realized that they had no choice, and adjusted to the spirit of the time, manifested in the Franciscan reforms which corresponded not only to the interests of the religious French protectorate, but to those of the Church as well.[75]

French apprehensions about the appointment of the patriarch were realized immediately. Patriarch Joseph Valegra came to Jerusalem on January 17, 1848, and was received with great honor. The Sardinian consul immediately became competitive regarding the traditions of showing respect. He challenged the established order, whereby the protectorate granted the French consul and his secretary the right to be first in line while the other consuls followed in the alphabetical order of the countries they represented. In addition, when the patriarch ceremoniously entered the Church of the Holy Sepulchre, the French and Sardinian consuls both marched beside him – the French on the right, and the Sardinian on the left. This clearly indicated the special position of the Sardinian at the expense of the Frenchman. The patriarch's patriotism made him supportive of the Sardinian policy, which aimed at an independent Sardinian protectorate to parallel the French protectorate.

Moreover, the Sardinian consul appealed to the Pasha to declare that the Pasha did not recognize the exclusive protectorate of the French consul over the monks of the Terra Sancta order and the affairs of the monasteries.[76]

The French position was decidedly opposed to this. The protectorate had never been shared, and would forever remain exclusively French, with no need for any partner.[77]

None of this, however, contradicts or negates the extensive religious activity initiated by the new patriarch. As part of this activity, he established Latin missions in Palestinian towns and villages where Christian communities resided, such as Bayt Jala (1853), Jifna and Lidda

(1856), Ramallah (1857), Bir Zayt and Tayba (1859) and Nablus (1862).[78]

Chapter 6

Rumors about Occupation

The turmoil and disorder (bordering on anarchy) which prevailed in Jerusalem and Palestine during this period, the weakness of the central government and its representative, the inability or unwillingness of the Wali to fulfill his duty as the sovereign's representative to protect his non-Muslim subjects in face of the struggles between the Qays and Yaman, the patriarch's intrigues and the struggles among the Christian denominations – all these clearly exposed the impotence of the protectorate in its existing format.

The yearning for a different, more effective kind of protectorate was expressed in the first half of 1848, in demands addressed to the government institutions in Paris by two elements representing two separate entities in Palestine:

1. A petition on behalf of the Terra Sancta order was presented to the National Assembly, requesting a more

effective protectorate than that agreed upon with previous governments (*"une protection plus efficace que celle accordée par les gouvernements précédents "*).[79]

2. The French consul in Jerusalem proposed that the French government should send to Jaffa the French ships that delivered mail from Malta to Alexandretta and Beirut. The British had also thought of this idea, and when the report was written, they were already waiting for the arrival of the first ship that would connect the trade posts situated along the coast (*"le Consul de France avait proposé au gouvernement Français de faire toucher à Jaffa nos bâtiments qui font la correspondance de Malte à Alexandrette et à Beyrouth... les Anglais ont eu la même idée et l'on attend de jour en jour le premier bateau"*).[80] Such a step would at least constitute a serious declaration of intent regarding a more effective implementation of the French protectorate.

As mentioned above, in 1855 rumors spread in Jerusalem of a plan for French military occupation. Was this plan devised in response to the petitions and the demands of the consul, or was it a far-reaching French plan? The British consul in Jerusalem, James A. Finn, reported in a document sent from Jerusalem on May 28, 1855, that due to the anarchy in Palestine and Jerusalem *"the idea of a French army of occupation"* had quickly begun to seep into the minds of the city's inhabitants.

The British consul reported that Prussian Consul Rosen had told him of a conversation held in his presence between the French consul and his secretary, in front of the Governor of Jerusalem, Kamil Pasha, in a language familiar to him, and intended for the Pasha's ears only. The gist of the conversations was that Consul M. Lequeux was making an effort to speed up the process of "bringing a French army of occupation into Palestine".

Moreover, according to the same report, "the Latin patriarch officially required", upon his "return last autumn from Jaffa, to be reinstated in his position in Bayt Jala, by a French military escort." The document also mentions that the French General Du Parc, who had been an officer in Louis Napoleon's army, had recently visited Jerusalem.[81]

The conquest plan may have been a local initiative of the consul, intended to spur the General to quick action, perhaps so that the news would reach the Sultan and move him to restore order in Jerusalem, or possibly the idea was suggested by the Latin patriarch of Jerusalem for his own reasons, as Moshe Ma'oz believes.[82]

We must not ignore the original protectorate plan and the timing of the report, written toward the end of the Crimean War. Since Jerusalem was a catalyst for the war, the protectorate plan may echo French policy associated with it.

The "religious policy" in France lost none of its strength as a result of the tolerance and modernization brought about by the French Revolution. "*Dont la politique religieuse en France ne brillait point par la tolérance et la modération*".[83] Before the French Revolution and since 1740, French ambassadors in Istanbul had been directed to act forcefully on the issue of religion and give it preference, and this did not change after the Revolution.

It was the first consul who saw to it that the 1740 Capitulations agreement was fully validated and authorized in article 2 of the French-Turkish peace treaty of June 24, 1802. He also intervened to have the Gat Shmanim Cave returned to the Latins in 1804, after the Greek Orthodox had obtained custody of it.

It was Napoleon's foreign minister who ceaselessly incited the zealous action of his representative in Istanbul, to regain protection rights over the Catholic churches of the Levant: "*reprendre et exercer dans toute son étendue le droit de proteger les églises catholiques du Levant.*"[84] Napoleon and the governments of Louis XVIII, Charles X and their successors did not deviate from this policy. Despite the official separation between religion and state, the leaders of France continued to view themselves as the heirs of its "very Christian" ("*Très-Chrétiens*") monarchs. [85]

There is no doubt that when France used the term "protectorate", it did not mean for it to apply to several dozens or hundreds of priests and monks, most of whom were of Spanish or Italian nationality, and none of whom was an Ottoman subject. Therefore those using "protectorate" for these clergymen may be using this term mistakenly – "*qu'il sert à égarer ceux qui n'approfondissent pas la chose.*" The protectorate had a much broader significance, related to "imperialist politics", which were soon enough manifested in the Crimean War. [86]

The Christians of the various churches in Palestine, namely Jerusalem, Bethlehem and Nazareth, fought during this period over custody of the Christian holy sites in these cities. [87] But for the European powers (Prussia, Russia, England and France) the issue assumed a different nature. It became a motive, if not a pretext or excuse, for political involvement in the affairs of the Ottoman Empire, and preparation of plans regarding the holy sites and Palestine.

Conclusions

In this essay I have tried to analyze the European powers' race for Jerusalem in the middle of the 19th century, its sources, causes and process.

In fact, this race is deeply rooted at least two centuries prior to this time and has never stopped. France and Russia were the dominant powers from the beginning, and these two powers stood behind two Christian communities that struggled for possession of the holy sites. For the opponent powers it was only pretext. The real motives, as we have seen, was the apprehension that the entire region might fall under the influence of another power and the desire to prevent this from happening. This race changed over time. It appears during various periods as a commercial, religious, political, diplomatic, economic and military race, among other descriptions, and continues today. The question of "why" can be answered simply – guarding interests at close hand.

Notes

[1] Peri, Oded, *Christianity under Islam in Jerusalem. The Question of the Holy Sites in Early Ottoman Times* (Leiden, Köln, Boston: Brill, 2001), 46.

[2] Moschopoulos, Nicephore, *La Terre Sainte. Essai sur l'histoire politique des Lieux Saints de la Chrétienté* (Athenes: N. Moschopoulos, 1956), 370-377.

[3] Popoff, Alexander, *La question des Lieux Saints de Jérusalem dans la correspondance diplomatique Russe du XIXe siècle* (St. Petersbourg: Imprimerie Russo-Française, 1910), 228-237.

[4] Tsimhoni, Daphne, "The Latin Patriarchate of Jerusalem from the Middle of the Nineteenth Century until the Present", *Hamizrach Hehadash*, Jerusalem 1992, Vol. XXXIV, 115.

[5] Ben-Zvi, Izhak, *Erez-Israel under Ottoman rule* (Jerusalem: Mosad Bialik, 1955), 332 (Hebrew); Mordechai, Eliav, *Britain and the Holy Land, 1838-1914: Selected Documents from the British Consulate in Jerusalem* (Jerusalem 1997), 15; Hough, W., *History of the British Consulate in Jerusalem* (Jerusalem: The Middle East Society, Oct-Dec 1946), Vol. 1, 4, 6; Schölch, Alexander, *Palestine in Transformation, 1856 -1882* (Washington: Institute for Palestinian Studies, 1993), 48-49.

[6] Blacas, the French consul, reports he left Jerusalem on 15 June 1717. Archives du Ministère des Affaires Etrangères, Paris, Quai d'Orsay (henceforth: MAE), B1, Correspondance Commerciale, Jérusalem, 1699-1717 (henceforth: Blacas Report); Wardi, Ch, *The Latin Patriarchate of Jerusalem*, (Jerusalem: The Middle East Society, Autumn 1947), Vol. 1, no. 3-4, 6-8.

[7] Shalit, Yoram, *Nicht-Muslime und Fremde in Aleppo und Damaskus im 18. und in der ersten Hälfte des 19. Jahrhunderts* (Berlin: Klaus Schwarz Verlag, 1996), 141, 142.

[8] Popoff, 243; *Mémoires du Chambellan Mouravieff*, MAE, Jerusalem, 1842-1847, fol. 444-454; Shalit, Yoram, 193-271; Masson, Paul, Histoire du Commerce Français dans le Levant, Au XVIIIe siècle, (Paris: Hachette, 1911); Philipp, Thomas, *The Syrians in Egypt 1725-1975* (Stuttgart: Franz Steiner Verlag, 1985), 91-108; Wood, A.C., *History of the Levant Company* (London: F. Cass, 1964); MAE, B1, Jerusalem 1699-1717, fol. 628.

[9] Church Missionary Society, Birmingham University Library, CM/065/76B Schlien's Reports, "Circular of a Project for the Erection of Palestine into an Independent State", Church Missionary Society Letters, Journals and Reports (henceforth: CM);

Public Records Office, FO, 78/1120, Finn to Clarenton, 28 May 1855, fol. 108-112; Ma'oz, Moshe, *Ottoman Reform in Syria and Palestine 1840-1861* (Oxford: Clarendon Press, 1968), 218, 219.

[10] MAE, B1, Blacas, ibid.; Neuville, René, "Heurs et malheurs des consuls de France à Jérusalem aux XVIIe-XVIIIe siècles", *Journal of the Middle East Society*, (Jerusalem, 1947), Vol. 1, no. 3-4, 3-34; Roger, Eugene, *La Terre Sainte* (Paris: Antine Bertier, 1664), 461, cited by Mana', 'Adel, *Fruh family*, MA thesis in Hebrew (Jerusalem, 1978), 40; Chateaubriand, François-René de, *Itinéraire de Paris à Jérusalem* (Paris: Garnier-Flammarion, 1968), 272-273.

[11] Schölch, 77-79, 119.

[12] Popoff, 88-89, 130; Masson, 18, 178-185; Simon, Rachel, "The Struggle over the Christian Holy Places during the Ottoman Period" in Cohen, Richard, *Vision and Conflict in the Holy Land* (NY – Jerusalem: Yad Ben-Zvi, 1985), 29, 31, 44; İnalcik, I., *Imtiyāzāt*, Encyclopaedia of Islam, III (Leiden: Brill, 1979), 1179, 1185 (henceforth: EI); Hurewitz, J.C., *Diplomacy in the Near and Middle East, Documentary Record 1535-1914*, 2 volumes, (Princeton, New Jersey: D. Van Nostrand Company Inc., 1956), 1:1-5, 25-35, 54-61; Gibb, H.A.R. and Harold Bowen, *Islamic Society and the West*, 2 volumes (London: Oxford University Press, 1965) 2:244, n. 2; Triaud, Jean-Louis, *La Correspondance Politique des Consuls à Jérusalem 1843-1878* (Paris: Université Paris VII-Jussieu, Mémoire de maîtrise d'Histoire, 1992), 40-43, 52, 54-59 (Document No. MT-2092, Bibliothèque IREMAM, Aix en Provence).

[13] Hurewitz, ibid., 1-5; EI, ibid.

[14] Albin, Pierre, *Les Grands Traités Politiques*; Recueil des Principaux textes diplomatiques depuis 1815 jusqu'à nos jours (Paris: F. Alcan, 1912/1932), 128.

[15] Homsy, Basile, *Les Capitulations & la Protection des Chrétiens au Proche-Orient aux XVIe ,XVIIe, XVIIIe siècles* (Paris: Librairie Orientaliste Paul Geuthner, 1956), 41-43.

[16] Ibid., 110-113; Simon, 19-25; Schlicht, Alfred, *Frankreich und die syrischen Christen 1799-1861* (Berlin: Klaus Schwarz Verlag, 1981), 148-150; Chateaubriand, ibid., 341-342.

[17] MAE, B1, 1699-1717, Blacas, 17 Nov. 1713; MAE, CC, Jerusalem, Vol. 2, 1843, fol. 9-10.

[18] Peri, 48-49, 150-153.

[19] Cohen-Muller, Rina, "De la Restauration au second Empire: quatre consuls, une seule politique (1843-1868)", in Trimbur, Dominique et Ran Aharonson, *De Bonaparte à Balfour, La France, L'Europe occidentale et la Palestine 1799-1917* (Paris: CNRS Edition, 2001), 46.

[20] Carmel, Alex, "Russian Activity in Palestine in the 19th Century", in Cohen, Richard I. (ed.), *Vision and Conflict in the Holy Land*, 45-49, 55; Ben-Zvi, Izhak, 332; Mordechai, Eliav, 15; Hough, W., 4, 6; Schölch, 48-49; Simon, ibid.; Homsy, 110-114, 152-162, 187-194; Bazili, Konstantin, *Memories from the Lebanon, 1839-1847: Syria and Lebanon under the Turkish Rule*, translated from the Russian...by Ari Avner, (Jerusalem: Yad Ben-Zvi, 1983), XIII (henceforth: Basili, *Memories 1839-1847)* (Hebrew).

[21] Simon, 26-33; Guerin, Victor, *Jérusalem on Histoire, sa description-des établissements religieux* (Paris: Librairie Plon, E Plon, Nourrit et Cie, 1889), 174.

[22] Ma'oz, 12-17, 187; Hofman, Izhak, *Mahammad Ali in Syria*, (Jerusalem 1963); Lewis, Bernard, *The Emergence of Modern Turkey* (London: Oxford University Press, 1965), 103-117.

[23] Polk William, *The Opening of South Lebanon, 1788-1840* (Massachusetts: Harvard University Press, 1963), 190-212; Ofeish Sami Adeeb, *Sectarianism and Change in Lebanon 1843-1975* (Ann Arbor, Michigan: UMI Dissertation Services, A Bell & Howell Company, 1996), 127-152; Ma'oz, 210-225.

[24] Marriot, J.A.R., *The Eastern Question* (Oxford: Clarendon, 1951), 233-242, 244-248; Guerin, 175-176.

[25] Ibid., 159-184; Simon, 34; Tazlor, A. J. P., *From Napoleon to Lenin*, Chap. 3 "Crimea – the war that would not boil" (New York: Harper & Row, 1966), 60-70; Guerin, 176-178.

[26] CM/065/76B Schlien's Reports; Moschopoulos, 237; Khazin, Philippe and Farid, *Majmūᶜat al-muharrarāt al-siyāsiyya wa'l-mufāwadāt al-duwaliyya ʿan Sūriyya wa-Lubnān* (Juniya: Matbaᶜat al-Sabr, 1910-1911), 1:11-115.

[27] Hajjar, J., *L'Europe et les destinées du Proche-Orient 1815-1848* (Paris: Bloud & Gay, 1970), 499, cites L. Lemmens in Girolamo Golubovitch, *Biblioteca Bio-Bibliografica della Terra Santa dell' Oriente Francescano* (Firenze: Quaracchi, Collegio di S. Bonaventura, 1922), 2:119-121.

[28] Moschopoulos, 239-242. Also cites Popoff, 223-227, Documents Nos. 126, 127, Mr de Werther à Mr de Libermann, Berlin, 24 Feb. 1841.

[29] Hechler, William Henry, *The Jerusalem Bishophic Documents* (London: Trubner and Co, 1883), 23-29.

[30] Popoff, 228-237, Document No. 130-133. Projet de dépêche à Mr Titoff, 11 Mars 1841.

[31] Ibid., 235.

[32] Moschopoulos, 371-375, Appendix No. 11, 12.

[33] Tuchman, Barbara, *Bible and Sword* (New York: Funk & Wagnalls, 1968), 150-174.

[34] Moschopoulos, 230-232.

[35] Laurens, Henry, *La Question de Palestine, Tome Premier 1799-1922, l'invention de la Terre Sainte* (Paris: Librairie Artheme Fayard, April 1999), 51.

[36] Ross William Collins, *Catholicism and the Second French Republic 1848-1852* (New York: Columbia University Press, 1923), 47-70.

[37] MAE, Jerusalem, 1842-1847, Vol. 2, fol. 9-19; Cohen-Muller, 46.

[38] Schlicht, 83, cites Douin, G., *La Mission du Baron de Bois-le-Comte: L'Egypte et la Syrie en 1883* (Cairo 1927), 178; Guerin, 390.

[39] Bury, J.P.T, *The New Cambridge Modern History* (Cambridge: Cambridge University Press, 1960), 18, 468-473; Homsy, 41-43.

[40] Hajjar, 484; MAE, Rome, Vol. 984, fol. 5-6. This project met with the opposition of the Franciscan Order, which up until then had represented the Church's interests in Jerusalem.

[41] MAE, ibid., Vol. 834, fol. 48-51.

[42] Simon, 25-26, 30-35; Carmel, "Russian Activity in Palestine", in *Palestine in the 19th Century"* in Cohen, Richard, ibid., 49-50, 55-57; Basili, *Memories 1839-1847*, II, 280.

[43] Hajjar, 485, cites Lemmens, ibid., 112-113.

[44] Hajjar, 488; MAE, Jerusalem, 1842-1847, fol. 7-9.

[45] Prawer, Joshua, "The Latin Kingdom of Jerusalem", *European Colonialism in the Middle East* (London: Weidenfeld and Nicolson, 1972), chapters X, XII, XIV.

[46] Hajjar, ibid.; Simon, 25.

[47] Laurens, Henry, *L'Expédition d'Egypte 1798-1801* (Paris: Armand Colin, 1989), 185, cites essay of Volney in *Le Moniteur*, 26 *Brumaire*, year 7 (16 Nov. 1798); Homsy, 186; Moiret, Joseph-Marie, *Memoirs of Napoleon's Egyptian Expedition 1798-1801*, translated and edited by Rosemary Brindle (London: Greenhill Books, 2001), 13, 20.

[48] Kobler, Franz, *Napoleon and the Jews* (New York: Schocken, 1976), 49-67, 72-76; Derogy, Jacques & Hesi Carmel, *Bonaparte en Terre Sainte* (Paris: Fayard, 1999), 339-343; see also Laurens, *La Question de Palestine*, 14-15.

[49] Moiret, 20, 23, 81.

[50] Halpern, Ben, "A Note on 'Ali Bey's Jewish State Project", in *Jewish Social Studies* (New York: Oct. 1956), XVIII, 284-286. This agreement was not validated since 'Ali Bey was replaced by Abu-'dh-Dhahab; Gelber, N.M., *Zur Vorgeschichte des Zionismus, Judenstaatprojekte in den Jahren 1695-1845* (Wien: Phaidon-Verlag, 1927), 30-31, based on *Literatur und Völkerkunde*, (1782), IV, Bd.8, 412-413. Gelber explains that it is not clear who initiated the project, the German officers or 'Ali Bey; John W. Livingston, "'Ali Bey al-Kabir and the Jews" in *Middle Eastern Studies*, (London: 1971), VII, 221, 225.

[51] Kobler, ibid.; Carmel, ibid.

[52] Tuchman, 150.

[53] MAE, Turquie, Correspondance Politique, 1843-1844, Tome 1, Jérusalem, No. 39, fol. 134, Lantivy à Monsieur le Ministre, 2 Jan. 1834; MAE Rome, Vol. 984, fol. 253-254; Schlicht, 181-196.

[54] Laurens, *La Question de Palestine*, ibid., 57-59.

[55] MAE, Turquie, ibid.

[56] Ibid.; Gouttman, Alain, *La Guerre de Crimée 1835-1856* (Paris: S.P.M. et Koronos, 1995), 85.

[57] Schlicht, ibid.

[58] MAE, Rome, Vol. 834, fol. 48-51.

[59] MAE, Turquie, ibid., No. 4, fol. 11, 29 Juin 1843; ibid., Tome 2, fol. 13, 12 July 1843.

[60] Ibid., Rome, Vol. 985, fol. 108-109.

[61] Ibid.

[62] MAE, Turkey, Jerusalem, 1842-1847, fol. 220-229, 274, 276-277 and Rapport de 2 Feb. 1847, fol. 412-415.

[63] Ibid.; MAE, Rome, Vol. 985, fol. 246-247; MAE, Jerusalem, 1848-1872, fol. 14-15; Hajjar, 495-496.

[64] Ibid., 501, 503, cites Lemmens, ibid., II, 136-138.

[65] Ibid; MAE, Rome, Vol. 987, fol. 72-73.

[66] Simon, 25-26, 30-35; Carmel, "Russian" in Cohen, Richard, ibid., 49-50, 55-57; Basili, *Memories 1839-1847*, II, 280.

[67] MAE, Rome, ibid., fol. 88-89.

[68] Ibid., fol. 129-130, 189-194.

[69] Ibid., fol. 176; Grant, A.J., and Harold Temperley, *Europe in the Nineteenth and Twentieth Centuries* (London and New York: Longmans, Green, 1952), 191-198; Corbett, James A., *The Papacy: A Brief History* (Princeton: Van Norstrand, 1956), 70-74.

[70] MAE, Rome, Vol. 987, fol. 88-99.

[71] Schlicht, 152.

[72] CM/065/76B Schlien Reports; Public Records Office, London FO, 78/1120, Finn to Clarenton, 28 May 1855, fol. 108-112; Ma'oz, 218, 219.

[73] Ibid.

[74] MAE, Rome, Vol. 936, fol. 327-328 and Vol. 987, fol. 23-24.

[75] Ibid., Vol. 987, fol. 176, 197.

[76] MAE, Turquie, 848-1851, Vol. 3, fol. 3-6; MAE, Jerusalem, Tome 3, 1848-1872, fol. 9-10, 14-15, 20-22.

[77] Ibid, fol. 9.

[78] Rogan, Eugene, *Frontiers of the Late Ottoman Empire* (Cambridge: Cambridge University Press, 1999), 124.

[79] MAE, Jerusalem, ibid., fol. 31.

[80] Ibid., fol. 24.

[81] Public Records Office, London FO, 78/1120, Finn to Clarenton, 28 May 1855, fol. 108-112; Guerin, 411.

[82] Ma'oz, 218-219.

[83] Gouttman, 80, cites Charles-Roux, François, *France et Chrétiens d'Orient* (Paris: Flammarion, 1930), no page number is given.

[84] Ibid., 80-82.

[85] Ibid., 73.

[86] Ibid., 83-84. Contrary to Triaud who concluded from the French consul's correspondence that "protectorate" meant only that the consul was obliged to keep all the Christians under French government protection, and to enable them to enjoy the benefits of the Capitulations. Ibid., 41-45.

[87] Basili, *Memories 1839-1847*, II, 293, 294, 297, 305.

Bei Fragen zur Produktsicherheit wenden Sie sich bitte an:
If you have any questions regarding product safety,
please contact:

Walter de Gruyter GmbH
Genthiner Straße 13
10785 Berlin
productsafety@degruyterbrill.com